Work for Play

Sharon Holt
Illustrated by Paul Konye

Contents

Chapter 1

The Idea

After lunch, Maribel was playing basketball with her friends, Theo and Valeria.

"Good shot!" said Maribel, as Valeria got another one in.

"Let's go on the swings!" Theo said.

"I don't like those swings," said Maribel. "They're too old. Valeria can't play with us over there either. Her wheels don't roll on the bark."

"That's okay," said Valeria. "Why don't we go over to the seesaw. I could watch you play."

"That seesaw's old, too," Theo said. "Just like the whole playground!"

"There's a new playground near my house," said Valeria. "It has swings everyone can use. I can play with you there!"

"We need a playground like that at school," said Maribel.

Mr. Carter, their teacher, was on playground duty. He heard the friends talking.

"I agree," he said. "A new playground would be great. But they cost a lot of money to build. Maybe the school can build one next year."

"We could raise the money," said Theo. "The school fundraiser a few weeks ago raised some money. Maybe we could use that?"

"I'll talk to the principal and see what she thinks," said Mr. Carter. "Then we'll talk about it later."

The school bell rang, and lunchtime was over.

Theo, Valeria, and Maribel went off to art class, happily talking about their ideas.

Chapter 2

A Class Project

The next day, Mr. Carter told the class about his conversation with Theo, Maribel, and Valeria.

"I talked to the principal," he said. "She thinks it's a good idea to update the playground, too."

The class cheered.

"I have a project for all of you," Mr. Carter continued. "Designing a playground actually fits in very well with the subject we've been studying in science."

"You mean simple machines?" asked Maribel.

"That's right," Mr. Carter replied. "Who can remember all the simple machines?"

Valeria raised her hand. "Ramp, pulley, screw, lever, wheel and axle, and … "

"and … wedge!" exclaimed Robbie.

"That's right! And a compound machine includes two or more simple machines," said Mr. Carter. "Now, I've divided the class into teams to brainstorm designs for the new playground."

"That sounds like fun!" said Valeria. "Let's get started!"

Mr. Carter gave the class a special challenge. He said that each group's ideas should include at least two simple machines. After a while, he walked around the room to see how the teams were working.

Mr. Carter stopped to look at the ideas from Katie's group. "Can you tell me about the simple machines you've used here?"

"Yes," said Katie. "The slide is a ramp and there's a lookout tower at the top. And this wheel will be really fun. You walk around inside to make it move."

"Those are great ideas," said Mr. Carter. "Good work."

Mr. Carter stopped at Maribel's group. "How is this team doing?" he asked.

"We're trying to come up with new ideas for equipment I can play on in my wheelchair," Valeria said.

"That's a good idea," said Mr. Carter. "Let's talk to the class and get everyone thinking about designs you can use."

Valeria smiled and said, "That would be great!"

Chapter 3

Something for Everyone

"Class," said Mr. Carter. "Valeria's group has come across an important issue. Let's hear what they have to say."

Valeria looked at her friends around the room.

"Most playgrounds are designed for people who can use their legs," she began, "but I can't use my legs. I can use my arms, but I need things to be at the right height."

"So we need to think about that when we work on our designs," said Mr. Carter.

"That should be easy," said Katie. "I'm sure we can include lots of things Valeria can use."

"Yes, I've been to playgrounds where I can use all the equipment," said Valeria.

"Sometimes even little changes to playground equipment can make a big difference," said Mr Carter.

"Like ramps instead of stairs," Valeria added. "And some playgrounds even have a special surface on the ground. It lets my wheels roll easily."

"That's a great idea," said Robbie. "We need to include a ground like that in our new playground."

"Some parts of it could even be wavy, like a mini-roller coaster," said Valeria.

"Wow, that sounds like fun," said Robbie.

Valeria then described the new playground she'd visited. It had plenty of interesting activities.

There was a tic-tac-toe game, and musical chimes to play with. There were lots of ramps to ride up and roll down, and bridges to ride over.

"It even has this cool swing with a platform," Valeria said. "I can roll my wheelchair right on and make it swing by pulling a chain!"

"I'd like to see that!" said Maribel.

"When we're thinking about the playground we're designing, we need to make sure there's plenty of interesting equipment at a lower level," said Mr. Carter. "Some of the things at the upper level need to have easier access for wheelchairs, too. So, let's get back to work and finish our designs!"

Chapter 4

Machines for Play

Everyone was excited when they arrived at school the next day.

"Good morning," said Mr. Carter. "I showed the principal the designs we came up with yesterday. She's very interested in the project. The school only has a small budget for a new playground, but she has found a company to provide the rest of the money we'll need."

"Maybe we could go on a field trip to look at other playground designs," suggested Theo.

"And we could look playgrounds up on the Internet!" added Maribel.

"They're all great ideas," said Mr. Carter. "We're going to be very busy."

Over the next few weeks, the teams continued to work together on their designs. They used the Internet to look at playground equipment and went on a field trip to try out playgrounds in the area.

The first playground they visited was the one Valeria talked about. It was specially built for children of all abilities.

"As you go around, make a list of all the pieces of play equipment you see," said Mr. Carter. "Tell which pieces can be used by people in wheelchairs. And tell which pieces use simple machines."

Theo pointed to a seesaw. "Look, Mr. Carter," he said. "We've found a lever!"

"And look," said Valeria. "This is the kind of swing I was talking about. I roll up the ramp, pull on the chain, and swing away!"

Valeria showed everyone how the swing worked. They all agreed it looked like a lot of fun.

Theo and Robbie tried the tic-tac-toe game. Everyone played the chimes. And Valeria had a great time steering along a bumpy path that twisted and turned.

The children found several other pieces of equipment they could include in the new playground. There was a set of monkey bars that was low enough for Valeria to pull herself along by her arms. There was also a tunnel she could ride through.

"We've still got two more playgrounds to visit," said Mr. Carter. "Let's see what they are like."

Children in wheelchairs wouldn't be able to use the other playgrounds very easily. One had bark on the ground, and not much of the play equipment was at the right height for Valeria.

"I see what you mean about playgrounds not being easy for you to use," said Robbie.

"That's why I'm so excited about our new playground at school," replied Valeria.

"Everyone will have lots of ideas for the new playground now," said Robbie.

Chapter 5

Machines at Work

Later that week, a builder came to visit the class. "Hello," said the builder. "I'm Mr. Peters. I'm going to help build your new playground. Mr. Carter showed me your designs. They were very interesting. I've tried to use an idea from every team."

Mr. Peters showed the class some drawings on a large sheet of paper. Everyone could see the design of the new playground and where their ideas had been used.

"That looks like our ramp and bridge," said Theo.

"There's our lookout with the flagpole," said Katie.

"And the matting will mean Valeria can get to the equipment easily. It will be a comfortable surface for everyone," explained Mr. Carter.

"First we have to remove the old playground," said Mr. Peters.

"All our parents are going to do that this weekend!" said Maribel.

"Sounds good," said Mr. Peters. "We'll bring in all our machines on Monday then."

"We know all about machines," laughed Valeria.

That weekend, the parents used sledge hammers, saws, ramps, wheelbarrows, and strong muscles to clear away the old playground.

Maribel noticed her father sawing an old pole in half. "Do you know you're using lots of wedges there?" she asked.

"Do you mean my saw?" he asked.

"Yes," laughed Maribel. "Those little blades are wedges!"

On Monday, after the old playground was cleared away, the builders arrived with their machines. The children watched as the builders used all sorts of machines to build the new playground.

"Look at that guy!" said Theo. "He's using the wheelbarrow as a lever to move that heavy concrete."

"That builder is using a drill," said Valeria. "That's a kind of screw!"

Chapter 6

A New Playground

Finally the builders finished. It was time to officially open the new playground. Mr. Carter used garden stakes to tie an enormous red ribbon around the outside of the playground.

"Those stakes are really wedges," Theo whispered to Valeria.

"And that ribbon is on a wheel," she replied.

The principal welcomed everyone. She thanked the children and parents from Mr. Carter's class for all their help with designing and building the new playground.

"Mr. Carter has chosen the class members who started the whole project to cut the ribbon and open our new playground. Come forward please, Maribel, Theo, and Valeria," she said.

Maribel, Theo, and Valeria came forward excitedly. The principal handed them the scissors, and they waited while Mr. Carter took a photograph.

"Did you know scissors are just two wedges and levers put together?" asked Maribel.

Everyone laughed as the principal said, "You all certainly do know your machines!" She continued, "You've all worked hard for this playground. And now it's time to play hard!"

Valeria, Theo, and Maribel cut the ribbon. Everyone raced past them. The three friends smiled, then raced over to join the others on the new equipment.

"How is it, Valeria?" Mr. Carter called out, as Valeria went through the tunnel.

Valeria looked over at her teacher. "It's great," she said, zooming through to the other side. "The most fun I've ever had!"

Levers

In the story, the children have been learning about simple machines.

The lever is a simple machine that can be used to help you lift things. When you push down on one end of a lever, the other end goes up. Levers can be used for work and for fun.

A seesaw is a lever! The weight of one person pushes one end down. This lifts the person on the other end.

A crowbar is another kind of lever used to help us do work. It helps lift and separate things.

Write a Description

Design a machine that would be useful in your classroom or school. Survey your classmates to get extra ideas about what the machine should include.

- Copy the chart below.
- In the first column, list the parts that your machine will include.
- In the second column, write what each part will do.
- Write a description of the machine. Use your chart to help you.

Name of machine: _____

Part	How the part will work

Think About the Story

In *Work for Play*, Valeria and her friends learn about machines and help design a playground. Think about these questions.

- What machines do the children think about using in their playground?
- Where do the children go on their field trip? What do they see and learn?
- What machines do the people who build the playground use?

To learn more about how machines help us do work, read the books below.

SUGGESTED READING
Windows on Literacy
Simple Machines
Wheels Around Us